Unit 4

Animals Everywhere

Mc Graw Hill Education

Contents

April the Agent

April is an agent. April can make
any dog safe. April can use her
nose to sniff so that no animal
can take a bite from a dog's dish.

1

David the dog had a fresh
bagel in his dish. But then
an animal took a bite.

David asked, "Who did that?"

April said, "I can give you a hand.
I am on the case."

April sniffed with her nose.
April did not smell cats.
April did not smell mice.

"It is basic. I think a dog
ate it," April said. Then she
made David's home safe for him.

David wanted to eat bagels now.
He had to carry out a bag.
David ate about eight bites of
his bagel.

"Our bagels are good!" April said.

"This case is closed!"

A Basic Dog

A dog is an animal that makes
a good pet. You can give a dog
just about any name you want.
You can name it April.

A dog can have little legs.
A dog can use its legs to do a
basic thing like run. A dog can
stand up and beg for a thing
like a bagel, too!

Give a dog a stick.
Can it carry eight sticks?
Some dogs can! But the sticks
can't be too big.

A dog can do many things.
A dog can pull on apron strings to
tell a cook that the pan is smoking.
A dog can fetch things for us.
A dog can romp and play.
A dog can be a pal.

May the gray snail likes to play.
May slides and glides all day.
One day, May had to carry mail.
She had eight things in that box.

Too much mail! May was about
to give up. Then May took a look.
Ray was an animal with a long tail.
Ray liked to swing and jump.

"Can you help with this mail?"
asked May.

Ray came and pulled the mail
with his tail. Ray took it and
placed it on top of May's shell.
May smiled at Ray.

May said, "Thanks, pal!"
May glided all the way home.

Now May stays and waits
for Ray every day. May makes
a trail. Ray gets May's mail.

Together, May and Ray say,
"We like our mail time!"

Tails

An animal with a tail may
do many things. If it is a fish
with a tail, it can swim.
It may swim as fast as a train!

13

With a wag, a tail will say when a dog wants to play.
A dog may not want to wait.
This animal will play at any time.
A dog will wag its tail on a gray day with rain!

Some animal tails can give pain!
A tail like this will aim and hit.
It will not be fun.

Some tails can get rid of bugs.
A tail like this will swish at bugs.
It is a big help to a bull!

15

Tails can be plain. They can
carry things. Tails can swing
and sway. Tails may just play.
Our animal pals with tails
can all do so much!

The Green Eel

Stephen Frink/Getty Images

Look! Can this be a snake?
It is flat from side to side.
It has two sets of teeth.
No. This is not a snake!

17

It is a fish. It is a green eel.
The eel lives in reefs and creeks.
It does not live in deep water.

The eel hides in rocks in the day.
It waits until the end of each day.
Then, it sneaks and hunts.

The eel can't see well, so it uses smell to hunt. The eel can reach into small cracks and holes where fish hide. It will feast on fish, blue crabs, or squid.

An eel has lots of big fangs, or teeth. It eats fish piece by piece.

Do other animals hunt green eels? We can't tell. It seems the green eel stays safe because of its big size and lots of teeth.

Clean Up the Team

The team came to play. They stood and looked at the small field. It was filled up with green grass and weeds.

Fox claimed, "This field is a mess. We can't run or play in it."

Sheep said, "I can fix the field. Just watch me go!"

Chomp, chomp. Sheep ate up all the green grass and the weeds.

The team ran and played. The running feet dug deep holes in the field. Then, the green field was a sea of mud. The animals looked at each other.

"We are a mess! We need to get clean," said Fox.

Ellie said, "I will clean you up." She dipped her gray trunk into the blue water. Then she sprayed each animal by the big tree.

"We are neat and clean," said Sheep. "Let's play again!"

A Doe and a Buck

These animals live in the
woods. A doe is a girl. A buck
is a boy. They must find food
to eat.

When it gets warm, a doe will start getting food with its mom. Mom will watch her babe grow. She will feed it.

Then a doe goes alone. It can go slow because it is still little. A doe will walk on its toes.

Paul E Tessier/Getty Images

What do these animals eat? A doe and buck eat plants. They can get food up and down low.

When there is ice and snow, a doe can eat wood. It may have to tiptoe over snow to get wood!

A buck can run fast. It may need to run in a field to get away from a fast foe.

A doe and a buck can grow up to be fine animals!

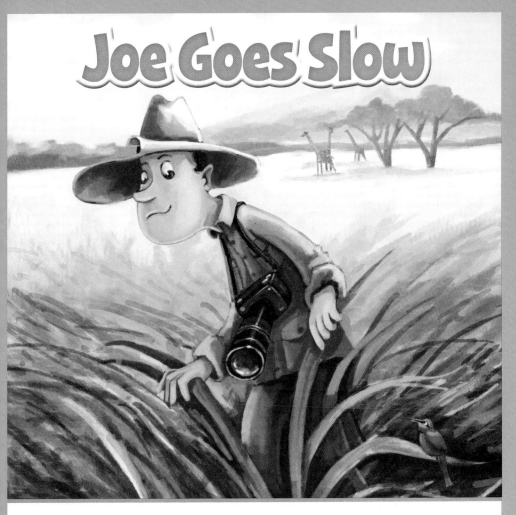

Joe Goes Slow

Joe is a man who likes to see animal pals. When Joe looks, he goes slow. He does not want to chase them away.

Joe sees a big cat! That cat wants to find food. Joe must stay low. He can peek over the grass.

The big cat can see a doe. This cat is a foe of the doe. The doe hops on its toes and goes!

Joe sees a black crow in a field.
The sun is warm on Joe's back.
The crow eats more and more
seeds. Joe wants to start to take
a shot, but the crow will not stay.

The wind blows Joe's hat. Joe goes
to look for it. He sees an ant. Joe
takes a shot of the ant! Joe is
glad to see his animal pals up
close!

Toads

A toad is an animal like a frog. A toad will start life as a tadpole. It is like a fish. When it gets big, it will find food to live.

Toads like to eat many things.
They like to eat bugs the most.

So where do most toads find
food? Toads can live on land
and in water. A toad can float
like a boat. It can dive under
water like a fish.

When it gets cold, toads
go under the mud. The mud
over them can help them to
stay warm. Then, toads can
rest and feel safe. Toads
will sleep and wake when
the sun comes again.

The goal for each toad is to live
and get big in a pond or on land!

So when you soak in a tub,
float and think more like a toad!
Have fun and do not get cold!

Joan and Elmo Swim

Joan and Elmo are pals. They like to swim and find food. They start each day by getting clean with soap. Then, Joan and Elmo swim!

Joan and Elmo swim by the coast. Elmo sees a big thing that floats. "Is it a goat?" asks Elmo.

"No, Elmo! That is a boat. We cannot eat it," she swims over to say. "Let's look for food."

Elmo sees a bug floating in the water. "I need food so much. I must eat that nice piece!"

"No, Elmo, do not eat that. It is a big trap! We are going to a place with more food now."

Joan and Elmo swim to a spot with lots of good food. The food is not warm because the water is cold.

Joan tells Elmo that he can eat.

"Yes!" Elmo said with a grin.

Jay Takes Flight

Jay is an ant. Jay does know how to go fast and slow. Jay can move things from the road. But when Jay jumps, he can't take flight.

41

Moe the Moth likes bright light. He flaps his wings high to reach it.

Jay asks, "Hi! Can you show me how you go so high?"

"No. Moths were made with wings. If you flew, you would be a moth!"

Bree the Bee likes to laugh as she buzzes around. Jay likes to listen to Bree as she buzzes. He says, "If you take me up high, I will get you a pint of milk!"

"I do not like milk," Bree said as she buzzed away.

Jay finds a kind ant with wings! He asks, "Will you take me up high?"

The ant smiles and yells, "Yes!"

Then, the ant caught Jay and flew up high!

Be Kind to Bugs

The sight of bugs might give you
a fright. If you were caught in a
spot with bugs, you might yell. But
be kind to bugs. Let's find out why.

45

You need more than a rake and hoe to grow plants. Bugs can help a lot. Bugs fight and eat things that can be bad for plants. Bugs seem to know the right thing to do for plants.

Carol Wolfe, photographer

If a bug flew into some teeth, you might say, "Yuck!" Don't laugh, but many people eat bugs and do not mind the food.

If you listen at night, nice bugs can help you go to bed.

Bugs can come from the wild or home. Bugs may seem bad, like a roach. But most bugs are good because bugs can help us a lot. So do not run and hide. Be kind to bugs!

Why Hope Flies

Hope liked to walk. She did not like to fly. She had wings, but when her pals were flying, she did not try. Hope was too shy to fly.

One of her pals said, "You can try to fly. When I tried, I did not know how. I had to listen to my mom. Then I flew fine!"

Hope replied, "I will fail if I try."

So a pal tried to tie a kite to Hope. Hope went up on her toes, but she did not reach the sky.

Then a pal caught Hope and picked her up. Hope grabbed an oak tree.

One day, Hope could see a pal,
Bill. He was so sad, he cried.
Hope tried to make Bill laugh,
but it did not work. Hope said,
"I know! I can try to fly up
on my own."

Hope did fly and Bill smiled!

Glowing Bugs Fly By

At times, you can see a glow floating in the sky. This glow shines like the sun. The glow comes from fine bugs that fly.

53

What do we know about this bug that glows? You may laugh, but these bugs make the glow from inside! That's not a lie! They like to fly in wet places, not dry. If those places were dried up, the bugs will find a new home.

You can listen and you may find that a bug is close. Just wait and look. If one flew by, you can try to tiptoe and reach up. It could take two tries. If you caught it, keep in mind to let it go free.

These fun pals are not like
most bugs. When one flies by,
do not run and hide.

Look at this nice bug. Do you
want to see it glow in
the sky?

Race Pony!

A woman named Holly came
from the city. She went to the valley.
She wished to get a pony that
would race fast.

The man told Holly, "This is a fine racing pony. Take him."

Holly got the pony to the racetrack. She rang a bell. It was time to race. Holly found out the hard way that it was not a fine racing pony.

The pony would not race. Holly could not find out why. What was the key? Was the track too muddy or the day too windy?

Holly tried oats. The pony still would not race. He was a fussy pony!

Holly met with Mickey, the jockey. He had a plan. He gave the pony grapes as a tasty treat. The pony ate them. Now, the pony races when it sees grapes.

Holly decided to write a note to thank Mickey.

Study with Animals

What can be easy for animals can be hard for us. That is a key to why animals can help us. We can study how they live.

We cannot dive really deep in the sea, but seals can. So we place a device on seals to check the sea. It sends back facts. The facts help us study the sea.

Dogs can smell quite well. That makes it handy for sniffing out wildlife that needs help. Dogs look in grassy hills and valleys.

Dogs have found animals that are not easy to locate. This helps people keep track of them.

Bats can help, too. Bats eat up flies near ranches. They hunt bugs that would eat up crops.

People write about the ways bats fly. Bats fly to places with no light. Studying bats may help people who cannot see.

DECODABLE WORDS

Target Phonics Elements

Long *a: a;* agent, April, bagel, basic, David

HIGH-FREQUENCY WORDS

about, animal, carry, eight, give, our

Review: any, are, come, for, from, have, he, help, her, no, of, out, said, she, so, the, to, was, who

A Basic Dog

DECODABLE WORDS

Target Phonics Elements

Long *a: a;* agent, April, apron, bagel, basic

HIGH-FREQUENCY WORDS

about, animal, carry, eight, give, our

Review: any, be, do, for, give, have, little, no, some, the, to, too, want, you

Snail Mail

DECODABLE WORDS

Target Phonics Elements

Long *a: ai, ay; ai:* mail, snail, tail, trail, waits; *ay:* day, gray, May, May's, play, Ray, say, stays, way

HIGH-FREQUENCY WORDS

about, animal, carry, eight, give, our

Review: all, every, for, help, her, now, of, one, said, she, the, to, too, together, was, we, you

Tails

DECODABLE WORDS

Target Phonics Elements

Long *a: ai, ay; ai:* aim, pain, plain, rain, tail, tails, train, wait; *ay:* day, gray, may, play, say, sway

HIGH-FREQUENCY WORDS

animal, carry, give, our

Review: all, be, do, give, help, many, of, so, they, to, want, want

The Green Eel

DECODABLE WORDS
Target Phonics Elements
   Long *e: e*, ee*, ea, ie; e:* be; *ee:*
   creeks, deep; eel, green, reefs, see,
   seems, teeth; *ea:* each, eats, feast,
   reach, sneaks; *ie:* piece

HIGH-FREQUENCY WORDS
because, blue, into, or, other,
small,
Review: animal, by, do, does,
from

Clean Up the Team

DECODABLE WORDS
Target Phonics Elements
   Long *e: e*, ee*, ea, ie; e:* me, she,
   we; *ee:* deep, feet, green, need,
   Sheep, tree, weeds; *ea:* clean, each,
   neat, sea, team; *ie:* Ellie, field

HIGH-FREQUENCY WORDS
blue, into, or, small
Review: again, all, animal, are,
by, her, is, of, said, they, to, was,
water, you

A Doe and a Buck

DECODABLE WORDS
Target Phonics Elements
   Long *o: oe, ow; oe:* doe, foe, goes,
   tiptoe, toes; *ow:* grow, grows, low,
   slow, snow

HIGH-FREQUENCY WORDS
find, food, over, start, warm
Review: animal, because, do,
down, from, have, her, little,
soon, there, they, to, walk, what

Joe Goes Slow

DECODABLE WORDS
Target Phonics Elements
   Long *o: oe, ow; oe:* doe, foe, goes, Joe,
   toes; *ow:* blows, crow, grow, low, slow

HIGH-FREQUENCY WORDS
find, food, more, over, start,
warm
Review: animal, away, does, of,
to, want, who

Toads

DECODABLE WORDS
Target Phonics Elements
   Long *o: o*, oa; o:* cold, go, most, so;
   oa: boat, float, goal, soak, toad, toads

*Previously Taught

HIGH-FREQUENCY WORDS
find, food, more, over, start,
warm
Review: animal, comes, do, for,
help, live, many, they, to, under,
water, where, you

66

Joan and Elmo Swim

DECODABLE WORDS

Target Phonics Elements
Long o: o*, oa; o: Elmo, going, no, so; **oa:** boat, coast, floating, floats, goat, Joan, soap

HIGH-FREQUENCY WORDS
find, food, more, over, start, warm
Review: are, because, by, for, now, of, said, they, to, water, you

---

eek 4 | **Jay Takes Flight**

WORD COUNT: 147

DECODABLE WORDS

Target Phonics Elements
Long i: i, igh; i: I, finds, hi, kind, pint; **igh:** bright, flight, high, light

HIGH-FREQUENCY WORDS
caught, flew, know, laugh, listen
Review: around, do, does, from, give, how, of, out, to, would, you
Story Word: moth

Be Kind to Bugs

WORD COUNT: 148

DECODABLE WORDS

Target Phonics Elements
Long i: i, igh; i: child, find, kind, mind, wild; **igh:** fight, fright, might, night, right, sight

HIGH-FREQUENCY WORDS
caught, flew, know, laugh, listen, were
Review: are, because, come, do, for, from, give, many, more, or, out, people, some, they, to, too, why, you

---

Why Hope Flies

WORD COUNT: 150

DECODABLE WORDS

Target Phonics Elements
Long i: y, ie; y: fly, flying, my, shy, sky, try, why; **ie:** cried, flies, replied, tie, tried

HIGH-FREQUENCY WORDS
caught, flew, know, laugh, listen, were
Review: could, her, of, one, said, should, to, too, walk, was, work, you

---

Glowing Bugs Fly By

WORD COUNT: 148

DECODABLE WORDS

Target Phonics Elements
Long i: y, ie; y: by, dry, fly, sky, try; **ie:** dries, flies, lie, tries

HIGH-FREQUENCY WORDS
caught, flew, know, laugh, listen, were
Review: about, are, come, do, does, from, new, of, they, to, two, want, what, you

***Previously Taught**

67

DECODABLE WORDS
Target Phonics Elements
Long e: *y, ey; y:* city, fussy, Holly, muddy, pony, tasty, windy; *ey:* jockey, key, Mickey, valley

HIGH-FREQUENCY WORDS
found, hard, near, woman, would, write
Review: are, could, from, her, now, one, out, to, too, was, what

Study with Animals

DECODABLE WORDS
Target Phonics Elements
Long e: *y, ey; y:* easy, grassy, handy, really, study; *ey:* key, valleys

HIGH-FREQUENCY WORDS
found, hard, near, would, write
Review: about, animal, are, do, for, from, have, many, move, of, out, people, they, to, what, who

HIGH-FREQUENCY WORDS TAUGHT TO DATE

Kindergarten

a	the	boy	happy	our	use
and	they	buy	help	out	very
are	this	by	her	over	walk
can	to	call	hard	people	want
come	too	carry	how	place	warm
do	want	caught	into	pretty	water
does	was	come	jump	pull	way
for	we	could	know	run	were
go	what	day	laugh	school	what
good	where	does	listen	should	who
has	who	done	live	small	why
have	with	down	many	so	woman
help	you	eat	make	some	work
here		eight	more	soon	would
I	**Grade I**	every	move	start	write
is	about	find	near	then	
like	after	flew	new	there	
little	again	food	no	they	
look	ago	found	not	three	
me	all	from	now	today	
my	animal	fun	of	together	
of	any	girl	old	too	
play	around	give	once	two	
said	away	good	one	under	
see	be	green	or	up	
she	blue	grow	other	upon	

69

DECODING SKILLS TAUGHT TO DATE

Short *a;* -s inflection endings; Short *i;* double final consonants; beginning consonant blends: *bl* blends, *cl* blends, *fl* blends, *gl* blends, *pl* blends, *sl* blends; -s (plural nouns); short *o;* alphabetical order (one letter); beginning consonant blends: *r*-blends; *s*-blends; possessives; short *e* spelled *e* and *ea;* inflection ending -*ed* (no spelling change); short *u;* contractions with '*s;* ending consonant blends *nd, nk, st, sk, mp;* inflection ending *ing* (no spelling change); consonant digraphs *th, sh, ng;* closed syllables; digraphs *ch, tch,* wh, *ph;* -*es* (plural nouns); long *a, a_e;* contractions with *not;* long *i, i_e;* plurals (with CVCe syllables); soft *c;* soft *g, dge;* -*ing* (drop the final *e*); long *o, o_e;* long *u, u_e;* long *e, e_e;* CVCe syllables; variant vowel spellings with digraphs: *oo, u;* inflection endings -*ed* and -*ing* (double final consonant); long *a: a, ai, ay;* alphabetical order (two letters); long *e: e, ee, ea,* ie; prefixes *re-, un-, pre-;* long *o: o, oa, ow, oe;* open syllables; long *i: i, y, igh, ie;* inflectional endings; long *e: y, ey;* compound words